THE EFFECTS OF ANCIENT GREECE IN MODERN TIMES

HISTORY 3RD GRADE
CHILDREN'S HISTORY BOOKS

BABY PROFESSOR
EDUCATION KIDS

Speedy Publishing LLC

40 E. Main St. #1156

Newark, DE 19711

www.speedypublishing.com

Copyright 2017

In this book, we're going to cover the effects of Ancient Greece on today's world. So, let's get right to it!

DURING WHAT TIME PERIOD DID ANCIENT GREECE EXIST?

. . . .

Thousands of years ago from 800 Bc to 146 Bc, Ancient Greece was the most important civilization in the Mediterranean region. The height of their civilization occurred before the Romans in Italy became powerful. Eventually, the Romans conquered the Greek empire and much of their culture was impacted by Greek culture.

The Porch of maidens

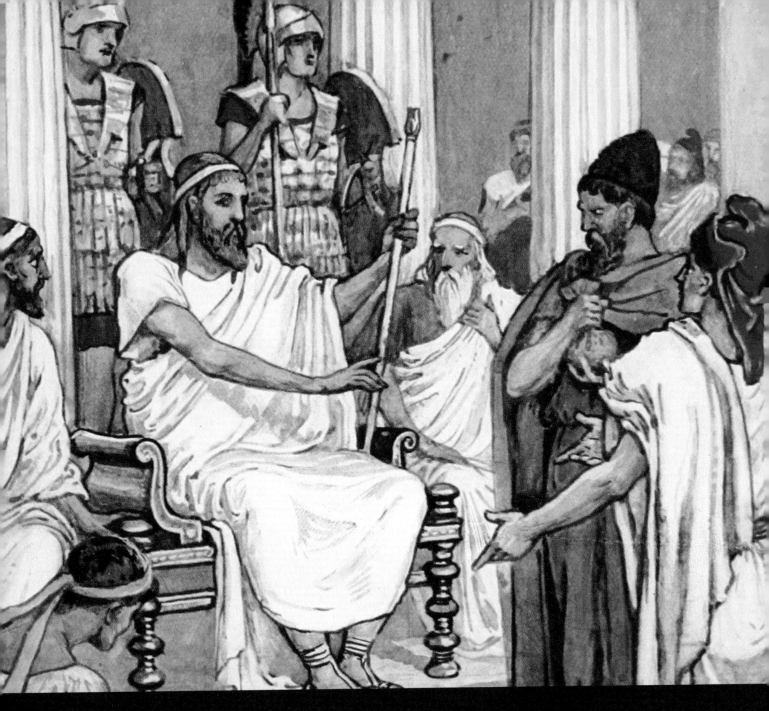

Solon the wise lawgiver

Western culture is built on a foundation of principles for government started by the Greeks. All the tenets of philosophy and the process of science originated in Ancient Greece. The arts, drama, and literature all owe their roots to this advanced culture. When Greek culture was at its peak, it spread across the countries in the Mediterranean.

Cultures are sometimes crushed when they are conquered, but that didn't happen when the Romans conquered the Greeks.

Ancient Romans

The Romans admired and imitated the Greeks by using their same gods, by copying their styles of architecture, and by using their language. They even copied their unusual style of reclining while eating!

Over 1,400 years after Rome had conquered Greece in 146 Bc, there was renewed interest in many aspects of Greek culture.

During the Renaissance (1300 AD to 1700 AD) it was brought back to life, in science, art, and architecture. This renewal of interest during the Renaissance ensured that the effects of Ancient Greece still have an impact today.

THE THREE PERIODS OF THE ANCIENT GREEK WORLD, 800 BC TO 146 BC

· · · · · · · · · · · · · · · · · ·

ℬ THE ARCHAIC PERIOD, 800 BC TO 508 BC

The Archaic Period lasted from 800 Bc to 508 Bc. During this time, the Olympic Games were introduced. The two epic poems written by Homer called the Illiad and the Odyssey were completed and forever influenced literature that would come afterwards. It was also the period when the first discussions about "rule by the people" or democracy began.

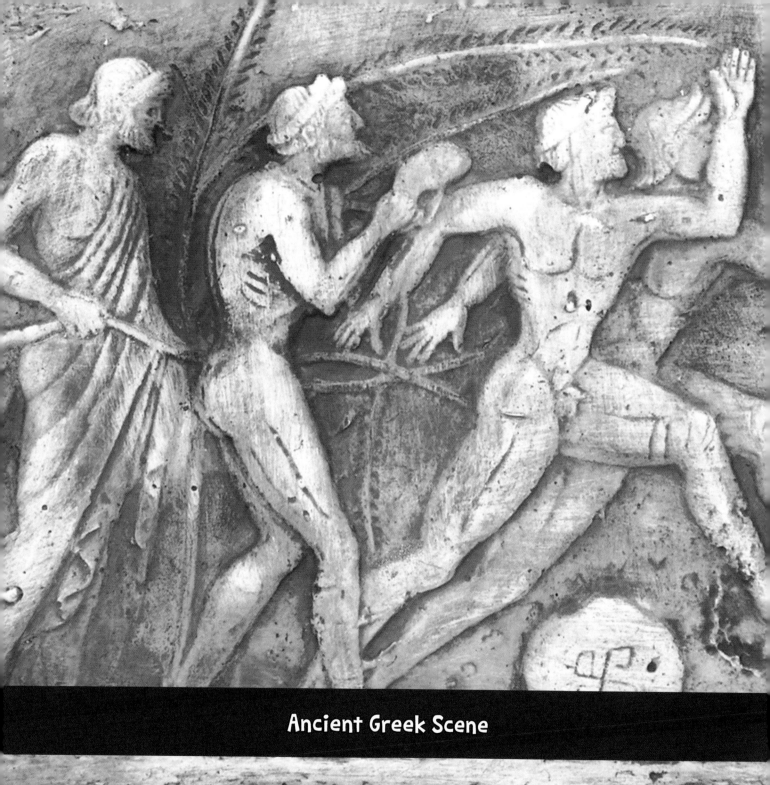

Ancient Greek Scene

ॐ THE CLASSICAL PERIOD, 508 BC TO 323 BC

The Classical Period saw the advent of the great philosophers Socrates and his pupil Plato. By this time, the city-state of Athens had a democratic government. Wars between the city-states were frequent and bloody. Alexander the Great grabbed power during this time period and started to conquer surrounding lands to expand Greece. The death of this legendary conqueror in 323 BC marked the end of this period.

THE HELLENISTIC PERIOD, 323 Bc TO 146 Bc

The last period of the Ancient Greek civilization is considered to be the Hellenistic Period. This period lasted from Alexander's death to the time that Rome had fully conquered their civilization in 146 Bc.

Romans conquered the greek civilization

Ancient Greek City

THE LEGACY OF THE ANCIENT GREEKS

· · · · · · · · · · · · · · · · · ·

The Ancient Greek civilization has had an impact on every facet of Western culture.

HISTORY

· · · · · · · · · · · · · · ·

An Ancient Greek by the name of Herodotus is considered to be the "father of history." It was his mission to record the major events of Ancient Greek history so they would be kept alive for future generations. Born during the Classical period, he was banned from his homeland of Halicarnassus.

Herodotus

Before returning home, he spent much of his life traveling, gathering stories, and recording them so that others would be able to learn more about the past by reading. Today, we feel that history is important to record and learn from, because of Herodotus.

MATHEMATICS

· · · · · · · · · · · · · · · · · ·

Some of the earliest mathematical theorems and proofs were written by Thales of Miletus. In today's geometry classes, students learn that an angle that is inscribed inside of a semicircle must measure 90 degrees, which means it is a right angle. This theorem is named after Thales.

Thales of Miletus

PYTHAGORAS.

Another famous mathematician, Pythagoras of Samos, created the word "mathematics." The famous Pythagorean Theorem of geometry is named after him. This theorem states that the sum of the squares of the legs of a right triangle is equal to the square of its hypotenuse. In other words, $a^2 + b^2 = c^2$ written in algebraic form.

PHILOSOPHY

. . . .

Pythagoras was a philosopher as well as a mathematician. In fact, he also coined the word "philosophy," which means "a love of wisdom." During the Hellenistic period, the leading thinkers in Greece began questioning the mythological religion that was part of their culture.

Socrates, his pupil Plato, and Aristotle all questioned these myths and started to seek logical reasoning and experimental scientific evidence to form the basis of knowledge. The role of wisdom and knowledge, man's place in the world, and the evidence that comes through human senses were all topics that took center stage. Their bold thoughts and questions had a huge impact on Western philosophy, as we know it today.

Ancient City of Greece

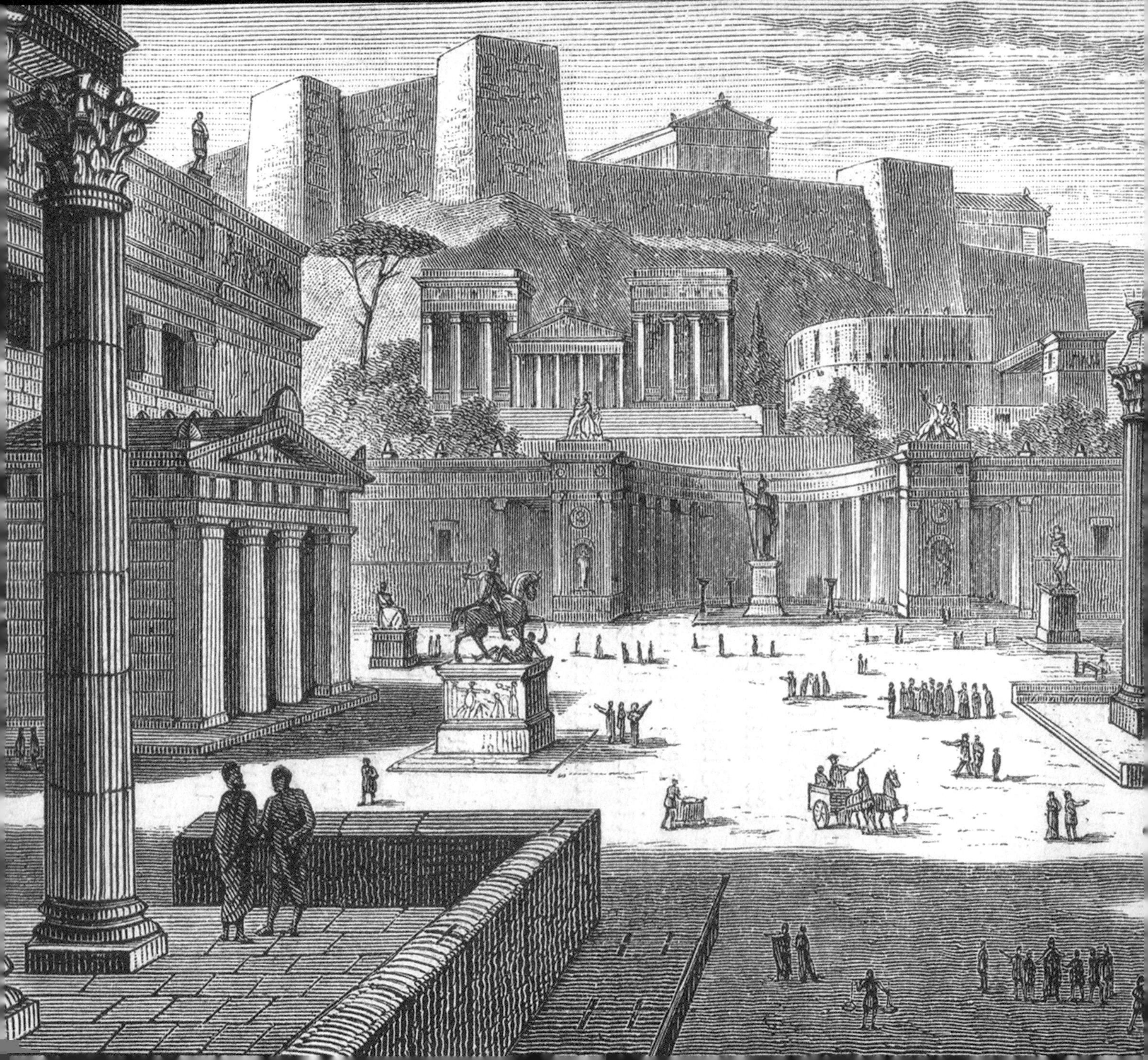

GOVERNMENT

· · · · · · · · · · · · · · · · · ·

The Greek word "demokratia" stands for "power held by the people." The city-state of Athens was the first to put democracy into place as a working government. This took place in the 7th century Bc (601–700 Bc) when the citizens of Athens were inspired by the successful government that Sparta had adopted.

A lawmaker by the name of Solon was requested to help find a way to assist the struggling majority without causing damage to the wealthy. He created laws so each citizen had the right to vote. Assemblies were formed to establish laws and ensure they were enforced. We owe our democratic government to these first steps taken by the Ancient Greeks.

Solon

TRIAL BY JURY

· · · · · · · · · · · · · · ·

Trial by peers is a concept that was created in Athens as well. Citizens could take each other to court, but the jury selected to help decide the case couldn't be chosen or influenced by the parties bringing the lawsuit.

The one major difference is that often these juries were made up of 500-1500 Greek citizens who all voted to secure the final decision on the case. The larger juries were enlisted for the most important

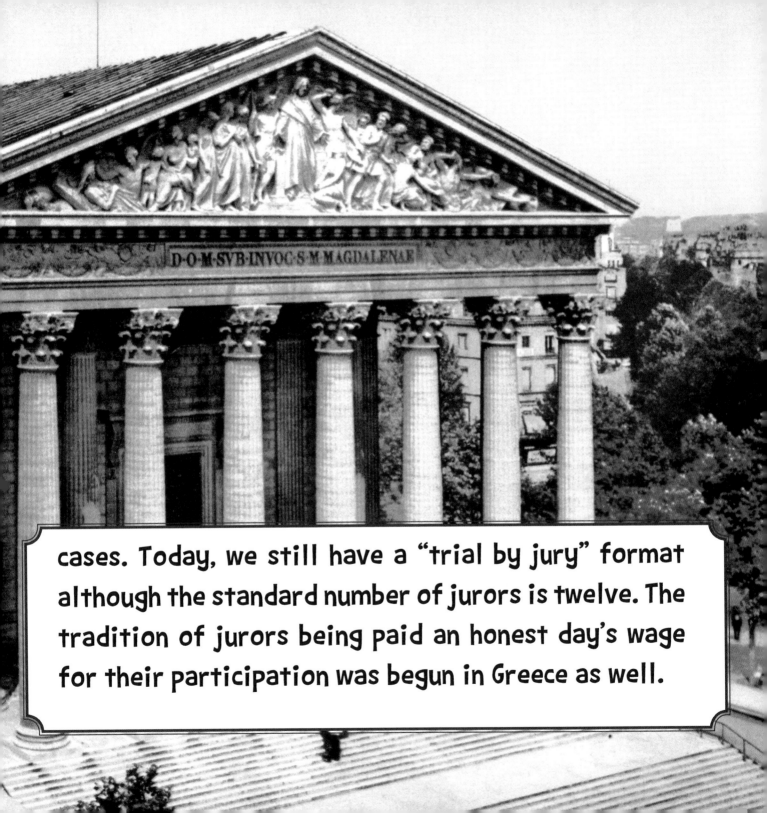

cases. Today, we still have a "trial by jury" format although the standard number of jurors is twelve. The tradition of jurors being paid an honest day's wage for their participation was begun in Greece as well.

The Theatre of Herodes

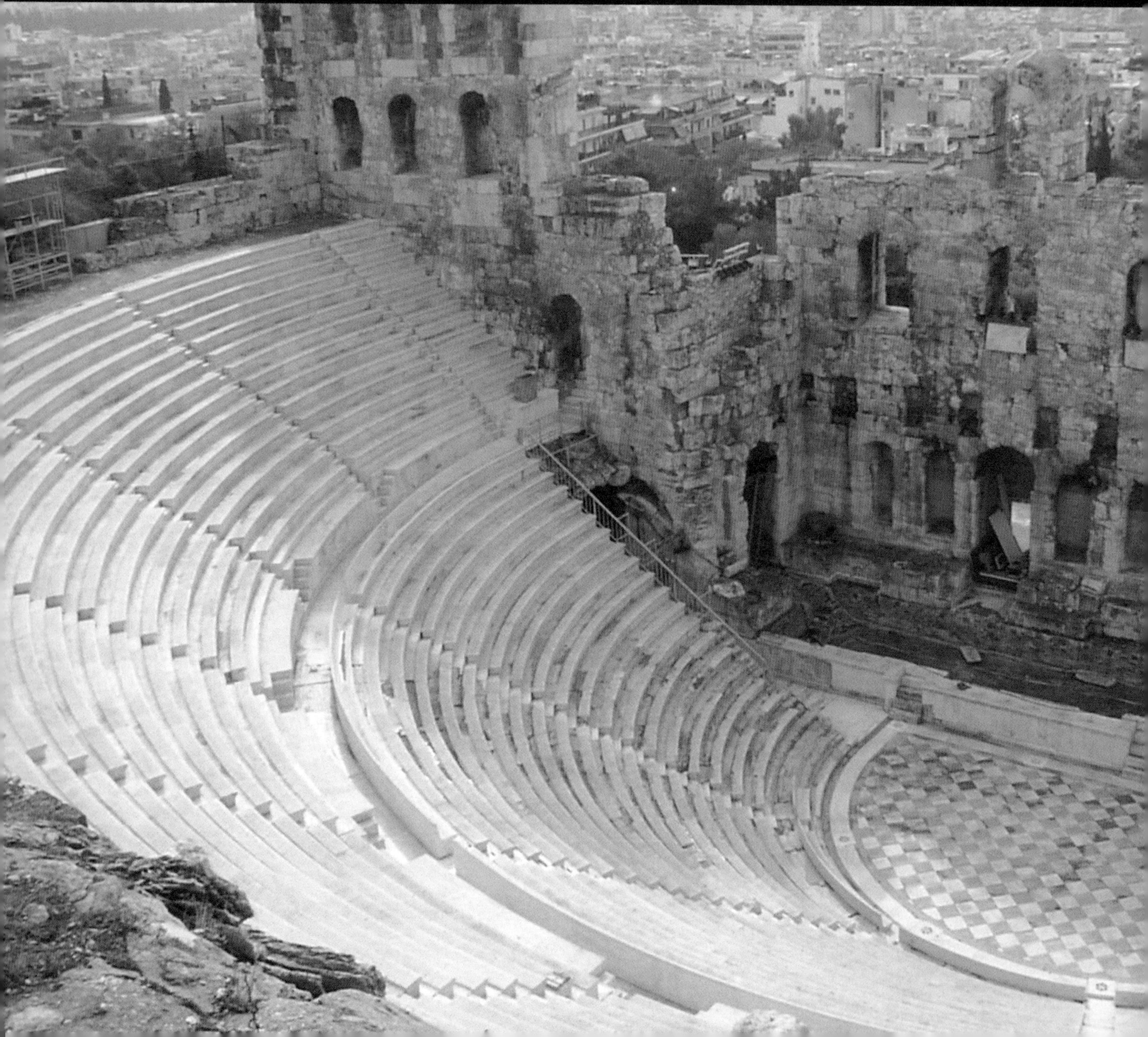

DRAMA AND THEATER

· · · · · · · · · · · · · · ·

The first Greek theater began as festivals honoring the mythological gods and goddesses. Then, there were dramatic poetry presentations where one poet would speak his poetry on stage to the audience. Eventually, these presentations involved into plays that actors would perform on stage. Both tragedy and comedy, which came later, were born in Greece.

Thespis was known as the first Greek actor and the word "thespian" comes from his name. The Greek citizen Aristophanes wrote comedies, which have still survived to modern times. The Greeks also had plays based on mythology with amusing scenes and surprising endings. These mythological plays were called satyr plays.

Thespis

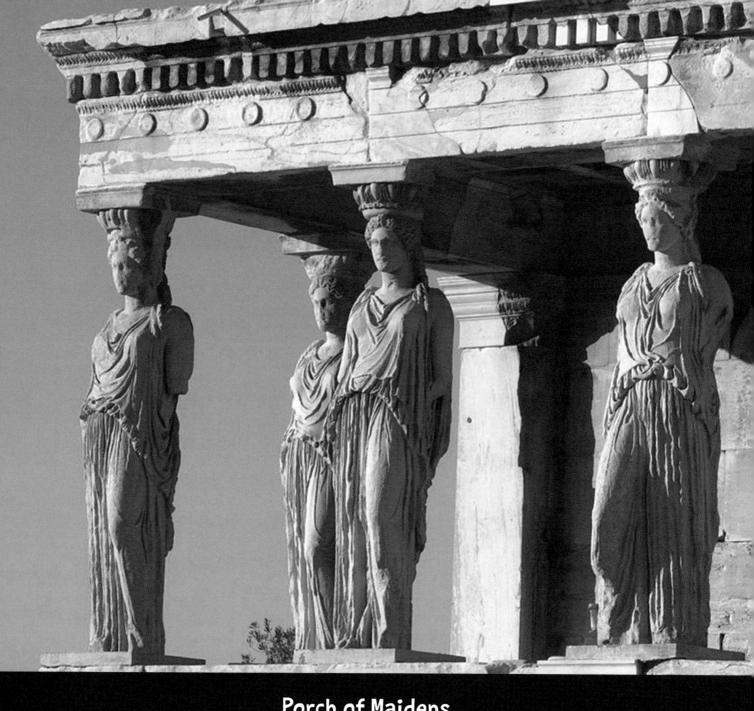

Porch of Maidens

ARCHITECTURE AND ART

· · · · · · · · · · · · · · · · · ·

At the center of Greek life was their belief in their gods and goddesses. They built great temples to their deities to express their devotion in a physical way. The Parthenon, which still survives in ruins today, is an example of their best architecture with its tall, beautiful columns and ornate sculptures.

Some of their temples had tall statue columns that would rival the complexity of any structure built in modern times. The precision of their architectural skill still inspires landmarks, government buildings, such as the U.S. Supreme Court Building, and elaborate homes today.

Sculptures were created as separate standalone objects of beauty as well and the Greeks were skilled in their carving of marble and limestone as well as their casting of bronze. They had their gods and goddesses for inspiration as well as critical historical events.

Pergamon Altar

NEREUS

Although their pottery was for practical everyday purposes, it was also painted with beautiful designs that today are presented in museums. Their styles of architecture and art had a huge impact on Western culture.

Astronomical Clock

SCIENCE AND TECHNOLOGY

....

The Greek letters are still used in scientific fields and the Greeks were responsible for many interesting inventions that we still have today. The first alarm clock was built by Ctesibius who was an engineer and inventor during the Hellenistic period. Until his invention, time was told using water clocks. He was also the first to conceptualize compressed air, which was used to develop cannons.

Odometers are tools that measure distance. There's some disagreement as to whether Hero of Alexandria or Archimedes is responsible for this invention, but what is known is that the Greeks used it to create roads and set milestones.

It was the Greeks of Alexandria who discovered the technology for the first thermometers for measuring temperature.

Odometer

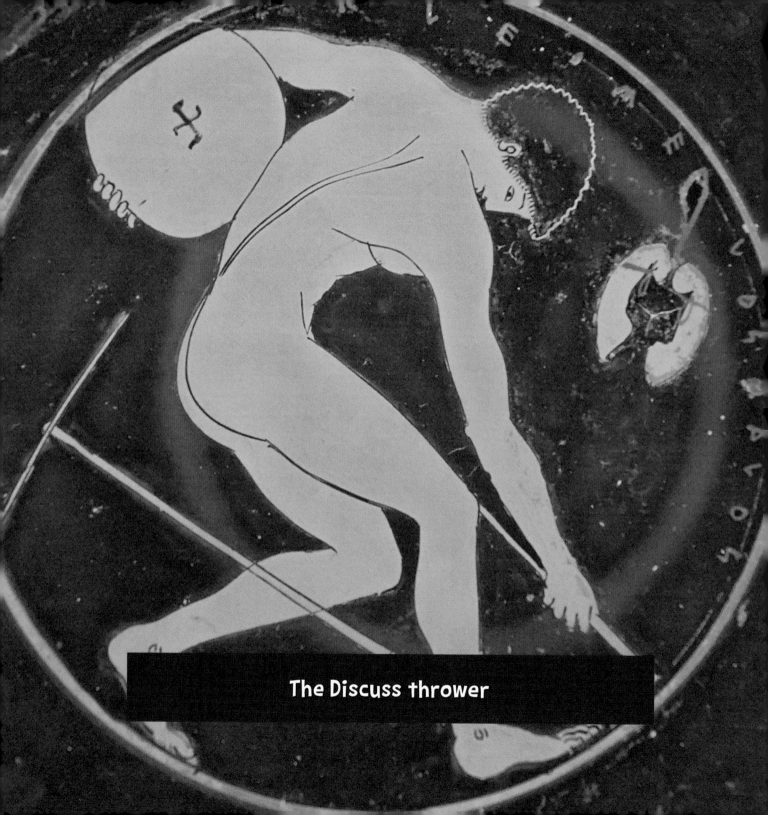

The Discuss thrower

SPORTS

. . . .

Over 3,000 years ago in 776 Bc, the city of Olympia in Greece was host to the first Olympic Games in honor of their god Zeus. The games took place every four years for a run of almost 12 centuries until they was banned by the Christian emperor Theodosius as a pagan activity.

In 1896, the modern Olympics was started and today this exciting event is continued. Countries around the world participate to win prestige and honor and carry the torch forward as it was carried in ancient times.

Sydney Olympics 2000

Awesome! Now you know more about Ancient Greece and how it still influences our world today. You can find more History books from Baby Professor by searching the website of your favorite book retailer.

Printed in Great Britain
by Amazon